MW00415260

The Profitable Charity

Accelerating Impact and Growing
Revenue through Charity Enterprise

AIMEE MINNICH

Editor: Mike Loomis
Cover design: www.MikeLoomis.CO

Italics in Scripture quotations reflect the author's added emphasis.

Details in some anecdotes and stories have been changed to protect the identities of the persons involved.

This book is available at special quantity discounts when purchased in bulk.

Printed in the United States of America

Special thanks to Lindsay Donaldson and William High for their significant contributions of ideas and research in early drafts of the book.

In my experience working with global business and nonprofits, charity enterprise has been quietly changing lives and communities. Every nonprofit leader should read this book.

—Tami Heim, President/CEO, Christian Leadership Alliance

Aimee Minnich challenges us to rethink what it means to be socially minded and empowering in our ministry endeavors. This book will move you to unleash innovation and creativity in addressing your ministry mission. I believe Minnich's ideas will fire the imagination of those who read it and inspire a new kind of ministry effort that will not only change lives but also generate the revenue to sustain the ongoing mission.

—Mike King, President/CEO of Youthfront and Senior Advisor at Museum of the Bible

Give a man a fish and he'll eat for a day; teach him how to fish and he'll eat for a lifetime; but invest in his fishing business, and buy his product, and he'll feed his whole village.

—Joe Knittig, CEO, Global Orphan Project

I've devoted the past decade of my life to spreading generosity because I love how it brings joy and intimacy with our Creator. God designed us to give generously from our finances, our time, our abilities, even our very lives. I'm excited about how the principles in this book allow business leaders to contribute more than just their money to the causes and organizations they love.

—Bill Williams, CEO of National Christian Foundation

Having worked years in the corporate world, as an entrepreneur, and as a nonprofit leader, I appreciate Aimee's solid approach and practical content. Most of all, I know this book will help elevate the lives of people around the world through charity enterprise.

—Jeff Anderson, Speaker and Author of *Plastic Donuts*

Contents

Aimee Minnich

INTRODUCTION

"The world is on the brink of a revolution in how
we solve society's toughest problems." —Social
Impact Investment Taskforce of the G8

On a sunny, warm March day, John sat across from me at lunch and
explained the sweeping capital project his charity planned to undertake.
They needed to expand their existing building to accommodate growing
demand for their programs. Growing pains are great, as they indicate
health somewhere in the organization. But as I pressed into John's needs
a bit further, my concern grew.

John's organization relies on donations to fill the gap not covered by
program fees paid by participants. His donor base was growing older
and prospective donors from younger generations weren't as interested
in funding his ministry. They were losing major donors faster than they
were adding new ones, and neither John's board nor staff had much
development experience. And now they were setting out on a capital
project that would require them to raise the equivalent of three years of
their operating budget just to fund their building expansion. Yet if they
didn't expand their building, they would have to cut back on planned
programs and potentially lose participants and their associated funding.
John was in a tough spot.

After six years of working with major donors at the largest affiliate
of the National Christian Foundation, I knew the difficulties of
fundraising for building projects. Many donors do not like to give to
construction of buildings because they believe their money would be
better deployed on programming. Additionally, many nonprofits forget
to consider the ownership costs of their new or expanded building when
embarking on the capital project.

John's story has so many common elements with other ministry leaders I've consulted with over the years, even those not facing a large capital project.

Does This Sound Familiar?

An organization struggles to meet fundraising goals for current ministry programs, struggles with donor attrition, wants to raise additional money for a new or bigger project, and isn't sure its existing fundraising team is ready for the big game.

Sometimes I hear frustrated executive directors suggest some of the following solutions:

"I just need my board to carry their weight in fundraising."

"If only young donors would understand our vision and why they need to fund our valuable work."

"Could you just give me the names of a few wealthy Christians who could fill the hole in our budget?" (Okay, I haven't heard that exact question, but the request has been implied to me more than once.)

"How do we use Twitter/Facebook/GoFundMe/a-new-giving-button-on-our-website to fix our fundraising woes?"

"Every month we put a blurb in our newsletter about planned giving, but no one seems to be calling."

Fundraising is hard work, and the process is becoming more challenging. There is more competition than ever for our donors' time and attention. Gone are the days when a fancy mailer and a smile-and-dial campaign would fill the coffers. There are more charities than ever vying for a share of donors' wallets.

The myriad ways to communicate with our audience are confusing. We know we should ask for planned gifts and wish we had more, but the pressure for current gifts is so great it's difficult to focus attention anywhere else. I'll say it again—fundraising is tough. Unfortunately, it doesn't seem to be getting any easier for today's Christian charities. For many ministries, the days of relying on recurring donations or legacy gifts are over.

Donors Are Asking New Questions

Most importantly, there's a growing sense among donors that charity alone cannot solve the most entrenched social issues of our time. I know so many good-hearted Christians who feel called to give generously of their financial resources, and have passion to share the Gospel, feed the hungry, take care of orphans, translate Scripture, end sex trafficking, eradicate abject poverty, provide clean water, and on and on. Yet, they've read *When Helping Hurts* and wonder if all their charitable giving is really doing the good they intend.

Consider Haiti as an example. After the devastating 2010 earthquake, there were more than twelve thousand charities on the ground in Haiti—more charities per capita than anywhere else on the planet.[1] And yet, the picture for most Haitians is still grim in terms of jobs, education, poverty, and sex trafficking. Charity aid in the context of poverty or crisis is essential, but it's simply not enough. The basic problem is straightforward: too much charity creates dependency.

We need a new model for fundraising. We need a new paradigm to achieve the impact our organizations seek.

Joe Knittig, CEO of Global Orphan Project, a charity engaged in orphan care and prevention in Haiti and Uganda, summarizes the new paradigm well: "Give a man a fish and he'll eat for a day; teach him how to fish and he'll eat for a lifetime; but invest in his fishing business and buy his product and he'll feed his whole village." Businesses built alongside charity have the power to change social dynamics in ways that charity alone simply cannot.

There's a growing awareness of this truth. Terms like "social entrepreneurship," "venture philanthropy," and "impact investing" have garnered much attention, especially among secular foundations and philanthropists. Unfortunately, the terms are not well understood and the principles needed for success even less so. One commentator says it well: "More than half of all nonprofits are engaged in some form of income generation, though few have the tools, knowledge, expertise, or desire to develop these activities into enterprises, thus realizing their potential social and [financial] benefit."[2]

Business and Ministry

In the late 1980s, before it was vogue to use the word *startup* my mom became the first employee of a new business. As the youngest of five in a financially strapped household with a single mom, I spent many hours at my mom's side while she worked. I went with her to talk with employees, respond to alarm calls in the middle of the night, visit bankers, talk through negotiations with lawyers, review marketing materials, and fiddle with broken copiers.

I know firsthand the personal sacrifices of starting and growing a business. I also know the inner drive that makes the journey fun and rewarding.

In the early 1990s, we were driving between my school and soccer practice when my mom got a call on her car phone. One of her former employees had opened a competing store just a block away from her top location.

When she ended the call, this squirrelly thirteen-year-old helpfully piped up, "Didn't he sign a non-compete when you hired him?"

She didn't seem to appreciate my counsel, but before she could compose an answer, I figured it out. "Oh, you got him when you bought that location and since he was already an employee of the former owner's, you probably didn't have him sign a non-compete."

I learned a critical lesson about acquisitions that day, but more importantly, I discovered that business was fascinating.

Fast-forward a decade and our family's financial situation changed dramatically when my mom's company went public. The IPO—often held out as the zenith of entrepreneurship—is a wild ride. I have seen the unique challenges and opportunities of family wealth.

When I moved from the private practice of law to the National Christian Foundation Heartland, it was motivated largely by a desire to help families like my own. I wanted to help other business owners and their families experience the freedom that comes through generosity. No matter how large or small, every gift given in surrender to the Lord is an act of worship. Every such gift can bring us closer to God.

Chip Ingram has said, "Generosity is a gateway to intimacy with God," because when we surrender what we have to the Lord of all creation, we get to know His goodness and provision in new ways. I will never tire of seeing the joy people experience through giving.

During my time at NCF, my role grew from staff attorney to president/general counsel. NCF Heartland is an unusual nonprofit in that it is governed as a charity and run with business metrics. I managed a staff to achieve aggressive growth goals, while working with nonprofit boards and their committees to make decisions. During my tenure there, we experienced multiple years with contributions over $200 million.

In the process, we coined a new phrase, *charity enterprise*, to describe the efforts nonprofit organizations were undertaking to add a business to their existing ministry efforts.

One of the most frustrating and rewarding experiences of my time with NCF Heartland involved incubating and ultimately spinning off our own charity enterprise called iDonate. I remember sitting at my desk, early in my time at NCF, and getting a call from my boss Bill High. He began the conversation with a question: "What do you know about private placements and capital raising?"

That began a long journey of spin-offs, reorganizations, capital contributions, donations, countless board meetings, calls with outside counsel, legal research, and on and on. iDonate now stands strong on its own as a full-service online fundraising platform for charities.

Because of these behind-the-scenes experiences launching iDonate, NCF Heartland became known as one of the only places people could go to get help with their charity enterprise idea. Thus, I have spent hundreds of hours consulting with these types of ministry businesses.

Nearly everything in the pages of this book I have learned the hard way. This book is my attempt to put in writing many of those practical lessons so you won't have to run into the same walls.

The book is for anyone who wants to understand the new landscape charitable finance, and see good work flourish with greater efficacy and sustainability.

What Is Charity Enterprise?

Charity enterprise is a profit-making endeavor that funds and complements a charitable purpose. It's not just a business that uses only its profits to fund ministry work. The business itself advances the mission. This model blurs the lines between ministry and business, creating social impact, while making a profit at the same time.

For some organizations, this means doing more. For others, it means doing differently. Charities and businesses can participate in joint ventures, and charities can develop revenue streams in their existing organizations or through subsidiaries. Influential members of the business community can use their wealth of connections, skill, capital, and knowledge to come alongside charities and join in a collective to move a nonprofit forward.

Increasingly, there are also opportunities for individuals and businesses to provide, or connect charities with, much-needed venture capital. We'll discuss real-world applications in upcoming chapters.

Because charity enterprise is a holistic endeavor, we can't truly engage in it if we bypass these essential components: the heart, mind, hands, or feet. In other words, we must address our internal motivations and external actions, changing them as needed. Thus, the label "charity enterprise" can be said to refer to an ideology and a set of methodologies, some applicable to nonprofits, for-profits, or both. In talking with many leaders in the business, ministry, and nonprofit communities, we realized that a specific prescription is impossible. But we can at least outline some of the basic methodologies and explain the curves in the charity enterprise road.

Leaders of nonprofits and businesses may adopt different charity enterprise methodologies, but they all see themselves, and their organizational contexts, as members of the body of Christ. Each and every one has the responsibility to do his or her part to display Christ's love for the world in one form or another. Charity enterprise is an additional, powerful way to reach people with tangible expressions of love—a love that delivers long-term value.

The challenges currently facing businesses, nonprofits, and ministries are very real, but we can work in sync as the body of Christ to realize profound change in countries, communities, and individual lives. It is our hope that these principles, stories, and practical insights inspire you to see opportunities for a new model for ministry: the profitable charity.

CHAPTER 1

IT'S TIME FOR SOMETHING DIFFERENT

"We all want progress. But progress means getting nearer to the place where you want to be. And if you have taken a wrong turning, then to go forward does not get you any nearer. If you are on the wrong road, progress means doing an about-turn and walking back to the right road; and in that case the man who turns back soonest is the most progressive man." —C. S. Lewis

I love to run but sometimes get bored with the same routes.

One early spring day, I drove to the edge of the city and headed out on a new route with my favorite running partner, Virginia the dog. I glanced briefly at the trail map on my phone and stepped into new territory.

It was a perfect day—sunny, not too warm, and the trails were soft. Virginia and I were having a blast. It was easy to follow the trail, and I quickly found my "zone."

Forty minutes later, I began to wonder why the trail didn't seem to be looping back like I'd expected. I ran a few more steps and realized, "This is stupid. If I've gotten off the original trail, continuing to run this direction will do me no good."

I checked the map and sure enough, I'd missed my turn ten minutes back. A quick left turn down a country road and two miles later, I was back on track. Thank you, Google Maps.

Like me, many charities need to pause, look at a map, and see if their current route will get them to their goal. In the work we do, it's easy to get caught up in the mechanics of charity and lose sight of the long-term outcomes we really want.

By relying on donations alone, many nonprofits are speeding down the wrong path. By only focusing on fundraising for today's programs and operations, many ministries are actually sabotaging the long-term impact of their mission.

It's time to do something different. The economic, social, and demographic pressures facing charities will require them to investigate charity enterprise as a significant source of revenue—and a transformational model to help people.

Stagnant giving with more competition

Every year, Giving USA releases a Survey of Philanthropy, reporting the amount of the nation's Gross Domestic Product that goes toward charitable giving. According to the 2012 survey, approximately 2 percent of the United States' GDP went toward philanthropy.[3] In 1971, the number was 2.1 percent. Some have called this giving rate "the stubborn 2 percent," because it has remained remarkably consistent over the last four decades.[4]

The changing demographics of wealth and philanthropy in the US will put further pressure on charities' fundraising efforts. Most of the donations that funded the growth of today's major charities have come from what demographers call the War Generations, born between 1905 and 1944, and the Boomers, born between 1945 and 1964. Together, these generations have been responsible for the vast majority of charitable giving in decades past. Because the War Generations are reaching the end of their lives, the Boomers are carrying most of the "giving weight." Since these generations are similar in size at the height of their influence (there were roughly 75 million Boomers in 2014[5]), overall giving has not dropped significantly.

The two generations following Boomers vary greatly in size: Generation X includes about 49 million members; Generation Y (Millennials), about 86 million.[6] For the period of time that Gen X, born between 1965 and 1979, dominates the workforce and giving world, charities will have fewer donors than during the height of Boomer giving. A smaller generation means less giving. And despite the enormous size of the Millennial generation, charities will not be able to rely upon this generation for giving in the same way as their elders. Millennials will bear the weight of unfunded government entitlements, meaning they will face increased taxes and less cash flow for giving.

Not only will there be fewer donations going to nonprofits, but there will be more competition for those donations. In just ten years, the number of charitable organizations in the United States has increased by 25 percent.[7] In 2001, there were "only" 1.26 million charities registered with the IRS, and 1.6 million in 2012.[8] Each year, people open more new charities than new businesses. All of these charities need to fundraise to meet their financial needs, but with stagnant giving, they will find it harder than ever.

Millennial Giving Patterns

It's not just the size of the generations that will change the face of giving. First, the diversity of these generations will affect *where* they send giving dollars. The Millennial generation is more ethnically diverse, including twice as many Hispanic members as the Boomers.[9] Barna research suggests that this generation sees a 43 percent drop-off in church attendance from high school through age thirty.[10] Barna offers a variety of explanations for this, but essentially this means that Millennials will not fund the same types of charitable efforts as their parents and grandparents.

Millennials are more cause-oriented than any generation before them and are less likely to draw a firm distinction between charity and business. Millennials recognize their buying power as a "consumer vote" and have different expectations of business and nonprofit. This generation's business education, for example, is increasingly steeped in social enterprise, sustainability, and corporate social responsibility. Furthermore, they make purchasing, investing, and giving decisions based on their ideals.[11] These attitudes can be an advantage for forward-thinking ministries who embrace and introduce the charity enterprise model.

As Generation X adapts and Millennials gain influence, this emphasis on sustainability is unlikely to stay within the confines of the private sector.[12] This means that the expectations traditionally placed on businesses will soon be placed on charities to a greater degree. The prevalence of social enterprise has especially caught the eye of the Millennial generation. Since Gen X and Millennials are loyal to causes and not institutions, they will exercise their power as donors and investors to support the best solutions to society's problems. So, if nonprofits are doing less for their cause than social enterprises, for example, those nonprofits won't be receiving Millennials' resources.

Socially Minded Businesses on the Rise

Not only are more and more nonprofits competing for a stagnant pool of donor dollars, but there are for-profit companies working to create a positive impact and deliver financial returns. These innovative entities driven by money and a social mission can broadly be described as cause-driven companies.

Ben & Jerry's is one of the most famous social enterprises. If you know them only as the makers of ice cream flavors like Cherry Garcia and Chunky Monkey, you may not know the company devotes an entire portion of its website, and a significant amount of its profits, to social and environmental activism.

The outdoor apparel and recreational gear company, Patagonia, is another prominent "profit for good" company. Patagonia has long been a leader for other corporations in its efforts to promote environmental stewardship and social responsibility. Both Ben and Jerry's and Patagonia have gone through the process of becoming certified "B Corps," a designation handed out by B Labs. More than twelve hundred companies, including Dansko, Etsy, and Seventh Generation, have joined the ranks of B Corps, committing to use the power of business to solve social and environmental problems.[13]

Whatever you may think about the causes these companies support, the fact they are seen as advancing issues that matter to their consumers has a lot to do with the success of these brands.

The increasing awareness among consumers that their product purchases have some charitable impact could, ironically, hurt charities in the long run. Millennials increasingly equate buying with giving.[14] Making a purchase from a company that is believed to do good work often feels like charitable giving. Much like sharing a ministry's social media post can feel like contributing.

Some studies suggest that by purchasing products associated with a cause, consumers are less likely to donate to charities.[15] As more and more social enterprises appear, consumers will have more opportunities than ever before to make cause-associated purchases. As a result, their perceived need and desire to give to charity could decrease. No matter how you view this trend, the changing financial worldview of these younger generations cannot be ignored.

The Charitable Tax Deduction

Another factor fueling the need for alternative revenue streams is the debate surrounding the federal deduction for charitable contributions. As the government looks for ways to narrow the enormous deficit, the charitable deduction frequently comes under fire because critics say it "reduces federal revenues by $54 billion, making it the fifth largest tax expenditure."[16]

If Congress were to limit or remove the charitable tax deduction, some experts estimate that giving to charities could go down as much as "$2.9 billion to $5.6 billion a year. That equates to eliminating all private donations each year to the Red Cross, Goodwill, the YMCA, Habitat for Humanity, the Boys & Girls Clubs of America, Catholic charities, and the American Cancer Society combined."[17] The potential for lost donations means charities need to get serious about looking for alternative revenue streams through charity enterprise.

With the coming changes in demographics and increased taxes putting pressure on traditional fundraising efforts, charities must look for new ways to fund their work. The solution lies in creating viable charity enterprises—profitable ventures that fund and complement the purely charitable aspects of each ministry's purpose.

Helping or Hurting?

It is not simply for the good of the nonprofit that we need to consider charity enterprise. The books *When Helping Hurts* and *Toxic Charity* debate the issues surrounding "too much charity." They make the case that handouts alone cannot fix the underlying social issues that contribute to poverty, fatherlessness, and related social scourges. In many instances, economic empowerment, which is much easier to say than to accomplish, will do more in the long-term to help those in need. It is a long and complicated endeavor to eradicate extreme poverty, and one that is beyond the scope of these pages, but charity enterprise provides an important tool for those striving to do charity better.

This is not to say that charity enterprise will replace donation-funded works. While there may be limited contexts in which charity enterprise will be the long-term solution, even those enterprises will likely need donations to get started. Furthermore, certain causes—like funding the local church and helping our neighbors with a short-term hardship—will always need contributions. To understand where charity enterprise fits within the context of donation-funded models and economic empowerment, consider a continuum.

A Continuum

On the spectrum of charitable giving, most people fall along these lines:

1. I own lots of stuff and use it all for my own purposes. I don't really care about the needs of my fellow humans around the globe.

2. I own lots of stuff but give some of it to others in the form of handouts, to meet some of their basic needs. (Too often, this becomes "helping that hurts" if done without regard to the underlying issues that created the need.) This type of charity, while crucial, treats only the symptoms, not the causes of poverty. Unfortunately, this is where too many of us stop.

3. I own stuff and use those assets to build economic engines that fund more charity (number 2) *and* give people jobs, training, and access to capital to build their own businesses. This is charity enterprise.

The Theological Thread of Charity Enterprise

Charity enterprise is not only warranted by the social realities of our day, but this model is needed in light of economic challenges coming our way. Charity enterprise is a way to live out biblical faith. Before we dive into the practical steps to charity enterprise, it's worth taking a moment to appreciate some important theological principles that support charity enterprise.

The Master's Minas

The parable of the servants and the minas found in Luke 19 is probably the most often cited passage on the topic of stewardship—for good reason.

In the parable, three servants were given ten minas—the equivalent of thirty months' wages. The servant who invested and increased the ten minas was rewarded, but the servant who hid them was not. The master took back his minas from the servant who hid his and gave them to the servant who had used his most profitably.

That confiscation seems harsh to most people. After all, the servant did not selfishly hoard the minas. He didn't steal or skip town with them. He simply protected them. Why then did the master respond this way?

Because the servant, out of fear of the master, did nothing with the minas. He did not honor the authority or expectations of the master. This story offers a warning to us if we fail to invest our resources of time, talent, finances, and even relationships, in advancing the Gospel.

In verse 23, the master asks the servant, "Why then didn't you put my money on deposit, so that when I came back, I could have collected it with interest?" Had the servant at least done *something* with the minas, even getting a meager return, the master would have been at least somewhat pleased.

But the parable doesn't end with the master scolding the servant. The master rewards the servant who did the most with his minas. The parable is about faith and effort. Actually, effort informed by our faith. We, like the faithful servants who believed Jesus's authority, can invest with Him in His work. We have the incredible opportunity to be a part of what God is doing right now in the world. He doesn't *need* us to join Him—but He wants us to nonetheless. He wants us to participate in the good He is working in the world, and we have plenty of reasons to want that too.

We Are Stewards

We are stewards of the resources God has entrusted to us. All of our resources—financial, intellectual, and relational—are our minas. And like the servants in Luke 19, we answer to our Master for the way we employ those resources.

As nonprofit leaders, we are stewards of a vision—to eradicate poverty in a neighborhood or region, to translate Scripture into every language, to end sex trafficking and the like—which means we have the responsibility to bring every resource and every good idea to bear in our cause. Charity enterprise gives us another tool in our arsenal and an opportunity to invest in doing good in the world.

Furthermore, charity enterprise offers donors the ability to deploy not just their financial capital in a particular cause, but also their business acumen.

We all know that generosity is about much more than money; it includes time and talent as well. I have often heard a business owner describe his frustration at not being able to volunteer his time effectively:

> I don't know how to help my church—I'm a terrible musician and can't serve on the worship team, meeting new people intimidates me so I don't want to be on the welcome committee, and the little kids are afraid of my beard and tall stature so I can't do kids ministry. But I feel like I may be finally figuring it out since my church launched a charity enterprise initiative this year. I have never felt so purposeful as when I'm bringing my years of business experience to the table to help create long-lasting transformation.

Charity enterprise can be a great investment of our Master's minas.

It Works: Case Study of Empowerment Exchange

The Charity: Empowerment Exchange is a nonprofit social enterprise dedicated to empowering women and their communities to rise above poverty through sustainable economic opportunities.

Rather than creating dependency on aid, Empowerment Exchange ("EE") takes a market-based approach to alleviate poverty by advancing entrepreneurial solutions rooted in the dignity and creative capacity of the individual. By focusing on poverty reduction through design training, job creation, improved incomes, education, and access to global markets, EE believes that, when equipped with the proper resources, women have the power to help lift whole families and entire communities out of poverty.

The Model: EE employed and trained women overseas to make handcrafted greeting cards for Mother's Day in 2014. The cards were sold in over twenty-seven hundred retail stores nationwide. In the world of retail greeting cards, companies incur the cost of production many months before they are paid by the retailers for those goods. This lag in payments meant EE needed financing to make its model work.

The Investment: Because they are building businesses to provide jobs, skills training, and sustainable transformation in the communities they serve, EE needed investment, not just donations. The innovative solution model attracted a donor/investor who made a *charitable loan* to EE. EE has made quarterly loan payments that replenish the giving funds of the donor/investor.

Aimee Minnich

CHAPTER 2

CHARITY ENTERPRISE—WHAT IT IS AND WHAT IT ISN'T

"I have been impressed with the urgency of doing. Knowing is not enough; we must apply. Being willing is not enough; we must do." —Leonardo da Vinci

Borrowing on marketplace ideas that have surfaced in other contexts, and improving on them, makes charity enterprise both brand new and retro.

Missions organizations have been working on Business As Missions (BAM), and Faith-Based Entrepreneurship for at least a decade. Academics have been discussing social enterprise and social entrepreneurship for decades, even if those terms have only recently been in vogue.

These terms float around with very little agreement about what they actually mean. The problem with using this terminology is we typically end up ascribing different meanings to the same terms or using different terms to describe a single concept. Additionally, some of the older ideas suffered poor implementation and created poor connotations in the minds of many donors. For this reason, leaders in both ministry and business overwhelmingly agree that clear definitions are needed for the concepts presented in this book, including a new definition for charity enterprise.

By using the term "charity enterprise" to describe one concept, made up of the ideas and methods presented in this book, we can engage in a more fruitful dialogue. Charity enterprise is not a brand new idea and it is not in total opposition to the ideas of BAM, social enterprise, and the like. The charity enterprise label does, however, bring clarity to this space and facilitate effective communication.

Social Enterprise and Social Entrepreneurship

Over time, the meaning of "social enterprise" and "social entrepreneurship" has become convoluted and their usage today may not resemble much of the original design. Accordingly, we won't try to narrowly define them—we'll just explain how charity enterprise is similar to and distinguishable from the other general concepts.

Social entrepreneurship is a *way* of doing charity. Characteristics of an entrepreneur—including innovation, creative problem-solving, leadership, and dedication to a cause—are also characteristics of a social entrepreneur. But the social entrepreneur uses these ideals to further some sort of social or environmental mission within the traditional charity model, using donated capital.

Charity enterprise, on the other hand, tries to solve societal problems with entrepreneurial innovation, but within a model of raising capital to build an economic engine that will fund long-term transformation and produce profit.

Business as Mission

Charity enterprise is also distinguishable from Business As Mission (BAM), as it tends to focus less on the economic development of businesses, and more on doing business in developing countries as a vehicle for evangelism.

One such business, for example, transports solar panels to mountainous villages in Asia. The solar panels provide lighting and heating for homes previously fueled by sooty stoves that caused many villagers to develop lung disease. The charity enterprise's workers are then able to engage locals in conversation and talk to them about how Jesus is the true light of the world. After three years, more than one hundred people have found faith in Jesus Christ, and two discipleship communities are growing rapidly. But this spiritual profitability does not translate into fiscal profitability, so the business is subsidized by a nonprofit and used as a vehicle to bring missionaries into the country.

This business is certainly what BAM is all about, but it is not an example of charity enterprise. Profitability, although sought, is not the first priority and usually not achieved. This lack of sustainability has frustrated some investors. One BAM and Kingdom Business investor wryly noted, "I donated so these businesses could lose money." For this investor, the ability to break even or make a profit in business is not about inflating the pockets of business owners, but rather is a sign that the business is being run with God-honoring efficiency.

This frustration with the unsustainability of many BAM and Kingdom Businesses proves the need for new terminology to aid our conversation. Charity enterprise is not about "losing money for Jesus" as one investor/donor noted. Rather, one of the core principles of charity enterprise is the need for nonprofits, and ultimately the communities served, to become financially sustainable.

Impact Investing

Impact investing, a term coined by Rockefeller Foundation in 2007, means the practice of investing in companies, organizations, and funds with the intention to generate measurable social and environmental impact alongside a financial return.

Over the past twenty years, a few leading foundations have laid the groundwork for the explosive growth in impact investing. Now, mainstream philanthropy is shifting from a grants-only model of deploying capital to a model where donors seek to use investment dollars for impact while earning financial returns. Charity enterprise, as a type of impact investment, is a part of this shift.

Not too long ago, people had just two lenses through which to view the private economy—something was either a business or a nonprofit. Today, those two traditional classifications constitute the ends of an increasingly crowded continuum.

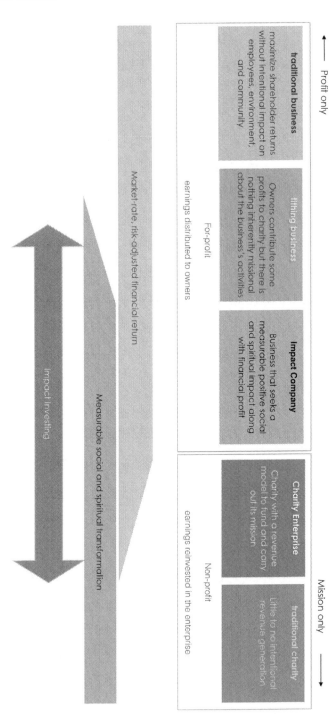

On the left, the focus of the enterprise is mainly (or solely) financial profit without intentional affects on employees, vendors, the community, the environment, or other stakeholders. Similarly, on the right, the focus is mainly (or solely) on the mission the organization seeks to address (e.g., providing clean water).

Somewhere in the middle is the sweet spot for impact investing, which we define as the practice of deploying capital for social, environmental, and spiritual gain along with financial return. These two types of return occur on different sliding scales along the continuum, shown by the gray and blue bars.

Financial Return

From left to right, the potential for financial return begins to decrease, starting with charity enterprise, a nonprofit which has a revenue model to fund and further its missions. As with nonprofit hospitals, revenue stays within the charitable realm to pay expenses or finance expansion. There are no shareholders, and private individuals cannot benefit from the activities of the nonprofit except to the extent of being compensated for their work.

With impact companies and tithing businesses, gross financial return prior to any charitable contribution should be comparable to similarly situated "traditional businesses." A growing number of companies, private equity funds, and foundations are out to prove how investors can experience comparable financial return through impact investing. At least one study supports this hypothesis. (Please contact me for the link).

Social and Spiritual Transformation

From left (traditional business) to right (traditional charity) in the diagram, we see the potential for measurable social and spiritual transformation beginning to grow with tithing businesses. A tithing business is one that gives a portion (perhaps even a large portion) of their profits to charity. The Newman's Own brand is a classic example—a portion of the profits from the sales of salad dressing and other consumer products goes to charity via the Newman's Own Foundation. While it's great how Newman's Own's success has allowed the company to give over $450 million to charity, there's nothing inherently good for consumers or the environment from the sale of K-Cups coffee pods or salad dressings.

The potential for positive social and spiritual transformation reaches its peak with impact companies. Rather than isolating the pursuit of the common good to a department or program, impact companies make charity an integral part of their business model, as with Co.tribute, Grace Family Home Care, or other similar companies we spotlight on our blog. These companies stay true to their commitments through carefully *defining and measuring* the positive impact they seek.

Where the gray and orange bars overlap—the places where there is both risk-adjusted financial return and measurable social/spiritual impact—is where you find impact investing at its best.

Why does this distinction matter? Because if we are not clear, or are unrealistic about our expectations of impact investing, their will be no success to tout and the movement will not catch on. We cannot confuse tithing businesses for impact companies and expect both to have the same measurable social impact. Likewise, we cannot expect charity enterprises, which properly have no investors and no private benefit, to have the same financial gain as tithing businesses.

CHAPTER 3

OVERCOMING OBSTACLES TO CHARITY ENTERPRISE

"The single biggest problem with communication is the illusion that it has taken place." —George Bernard Shaw

It's only been ten minutes, I thought, *and people are getting jittery.* I invited leaders in business and in ministry to a discussion so we could sit around the same table and talk about the future. Almost immediately, the discussion moved to collaboration between business and ministry leaders. What transpired over the course of the afternoon was a lively volley amongst the attendees.

"*Profit* and *competition* aren't curse words."

"But coming from a ministry background . . ."

"Why would you ever settle for break-even when you could be making a profit?"

"Mission can't take a backseat to the profit motive . . ."

"But if ministry-minded nonprofits aren't sufficiently motivated to make money, they are unlikely to succeed."

As each one began to share his or her experiences, one takeaway became clear: whether coming from the business world, the ministry world, or both, everyone was frustrated! Communication between the two was difficult, to say the least. A week later, I led another roundtable discussion to hear from others in business and ministry, and more than anything that meeting again confirmed: there's a rift and we need to do something about it.

What Causes the Collision between Ministry and Business?

The problem is not that we are unwilling to work together, or that we're determined to undercut one another. The problem is a lack of understanding. To overcome it, we do not need every person with an MBA to go to seminary, or every ministry leader to start prepping for the GMAT. But we do need to better appreciate each other's perspectives and acknowledge the fears and frustrations.

Thus, the following section contains a description of the thoughts and feelings many in the business and ministry communities have articulated during the course of our research, and in my years advising nonprofits.

Thoughts from inside the Business World

Businesspeople often feel like their pragmatism is not appreciated. They approach problems practically and thus speak in practical terms. Sometimes beautiful ideas are impossible to execute or too costly to reasonably pursue, but pointing that out in a nonprofit board meeting has resulted in being labeled "negative" or "uncompassionate." Many have felt the need to defend their motives as pure in the face of accusations to the contrary.

Just because a businessperson may be intent on evaluating marketing strategies and projecting profits doesn't mean they care less about doing good. In fact, many believe their business acumen helps them to do *more* good. They want others to know that their decision to pursue what works is not the same as a decision to pursue what works at any cost.

Every businessperson we encountered articulated some desire to be on the same team as those with ministry backgrounds, yet some of them had experienced rejection.

Thoughts from inside the Ministry World

Many in the ministry world have felt a lack of acceptance too. They seek intangible returns on investment that often do not manifest immediately. For those in ministry in particular, it can be challenging to explain their long-term timetable, either because they seek eternal goals or because social advances take years and even decades to accomplish. People involved in charity work also fear the pursuit of profit will cause "mission creep," or a distancing from the social or religious purpose of the organization. Although they don't see every profit-making effort as evil, some bad-apple businesses have spoiled the perception of commerce for many nonprofit leaders.

Why Does This Collision Need to Be Addressed?

We've built a false dichotomy between mission and profit. We assume that if someone wants to do good in the world (spread the Gospel, feed the hungry, take care of orphans, end human trafficking), they have to join a nonprofit organization.

The corollary to this (bad) idea is the equally wrong notion that if someone works for a nonprofit organization, they know nothing about efficiency, hard work, or the disciplines by which businesses live and die. And both of these ideas are wrong.

Neither sector has it all. Neither the "business" community nor the "ministry" community has all the vision. No *one* can ask all the right questions. No *one* has all the right answers. No *one* has all the necessary skills and experience. For any venture to be successful, vision, questions, answers, skills, and experiences must be brought to the table by people of different backgrounds, with different perspectives.

Toward Cooperation

Charity enterprise requires us, as leaders in business and in ministry, to work together well. Arrogance and ignorance, whether real or merely perceived, have created a rift between these two groups. The chasm is one that needs to be bridged, and is certainly one that *can* be bridged—we just have to start building.

We begin with a willingness to notice our biases and adjust our thinking if necessary. In general, there are three significant shifts for people to make when working with "people from the other side."

Distinguish between the Profit Motive and Greed

People in the nonprofit world sometimes object to profit and commerce on the belief that "money is the root of all evil." The verse many of them point to is I Timothy 6:10. But on closer inspection, the verse does not say, "money is bad." It says, "The *love* of money is the root of all evil."[18] Whether using King James Version, New King James Version, New International Version, American Standard Version, or English Standard Version, they all specify that it is the *love* of money that is the root—not the money itself.

Sometimes we are afraid the pursuit of profit will drown out our efforts to ignite social and eternal transformation. This may be a legitimate fear if taken to an extreme, but with clear expectations and ground rules, charity enterprise can earn money without sacrificing ministry outcomes.

Don't Discount the Intangibles

I once heard a board member interrupt the executive director's presentation on her organization's impact during a meeting: "This squishy ministry stuff is nice, but let's get to the 'real work' and look at the financials."

Unfortunately, this director isn't alone in his wrong-headed thinking. We should not dismiss the social and spiritual goals we seek simply because they are difficult to quantify. Our goal may be to improve the emotional and spiritual well-being of a community, change the business climate, operate an animal shelter, or tutor children after school. People at the table must acknowledge the importance of each of these goals and be willing to acknowledge the priority placed on those goals by others.

A ministry background doesn't imply lack of business skill. Unfortunately, many people assume those working in ministry lack discipline and drive.

Embrace a Culture of Accountability

Piggy-backing on the last cognitive bias, a charity enterprise that successfully blends the best of business and nonprofit culture will work hard to set goals and measure progress toward them. This can be fairly straightforward, even if it isn't easy, on the business side of the charity enterprise.

For example, if you open a thrift store, you know you need to measure foot traffic, profitability per square foot, and the other basics of the retail business. But when it comes to the intangibles, many nonprofit leaders are nervous, and rightly so, about goal-setting and measurements. It can be difficult, and even dangerously prone to manipulation, to measure intangibles like spiritual decisions and other intangibles. After all, only God sees the heart (I Samuel 16:7). And how could we possibly "measure" the work of the Holy Spirit, which is like the wind that "blows wherever it pleases" (John 3:8)?

All of this is true, but there is much good to be gained from measuring all impacts as the information can tell us where to plant more "seed," where to adjust our approach, and where to lean into prayer.

Triple Bottom Line

One successful business owner—we will call him Pat—has developed a model for his businesses as triple-bottom-line companies. This means he looks to create social and eternal impact along with financial return.

While these wouldn't technically be considered charity enterprises, I think his paradigm could be helpful here. Pat owns four operating companies, including one manufacturing business that operates inside a prison. He pays more than minimum wage, whereas inmates would make only forty-five cents per day in a traditional prison job. The state takes a percentage of their wages to help fund the prison—a social good. Plus, Pat's employees are able to help provide financially for their families.

Finally, Pat and his management team spend time teaching the men leadership skills, lessons on how to be a better husband and father, and even start Bible studies and discipleship groups in the prison. But for the fact the prison is a state-run entity instead of a nonprofit ministry, this would be a perfect example of charity enterprise.

Pat has developed a written plan for the profitability of his business, as well as for the social and spiritual outcomes he seeks. As for measurement, Pat says, "We measure outcomes when it comes to finances and effort on the social and spiritual aspects." For Pat, this means tracking attendance at the leadership and parenting classes his staff and volunteers teach. They also keep count of the number of Bible studies and discipleship groups going among his employees. A similar paradigm could be helpful for others in the context of charity enterprises.

First, determine what social and spiritual goals your enterprise seeks. These may seem obvious for a charity enterprise begun as an outgrowth of an existing ministry. It is still worthwhile to document those goals with as much specificity as possible. As they come to pass, the team can celebrate and give thanks to the One who made it possible.

Next, develop a plan to reach those goals. Because social and spiritual impact is *squishy* and depends on behavior changes in people, it generally takes longer to realize than financial profit. This is normal and should be anticipated. Likewise, a charity enterprise should hold loosely to the plans it makes for these two bottom lines. The human element may necessitate shifting the plan as your team learns more about what it takes to be successful in its endeavor.

Finally, regularly measure *and* report the effort of your team to reach those goals. This step is the easiest to implement, the most critical to long-term success, and also the most likely to be ignored. As Patrick Lencioni explained in *The Five Dysfunctions of a Team*, lack of accountability in a team creates resentment among team members who have different standards of performance, encourages mediocrity, missed deadlines and key deliverables, and places an undue burden on the team leader as the sole source of discipline.

Long-term success of a charity enterprise team involves bringing the best of business—measurement and accountability—together with the best of nonprofit planning and execution on social and spiritual impact goals.

CHAPTER 4

GETTING STARTED IN A STRUCTURE THAT SUPPORTS SUCCESS

"Plans fail for lack of counsel, but with many advisers they succeed."
—King Solomon (Proverbs 15:22)

Mike and Beth survived financial crisis, lost marriages, experienced a life-threatening brain hemorrhage, and in the process of navigating these challenges, found the saving love of Jesus Christ.

No longer content with the perfect house, the best grown-up toys, and business success, Mike and Beth wanted more—a life more impactful and fulfilling. Their quest for a richer life started in 2003 with a $750 check destined for a small shanty housing seventeen orphans on the Thai/Myanmar border.

A few months after the small orphanage opened, Mike chose to do something even more profound. He packed his bags and flew to South Asia to visit the home with a vision to bring a few friends into the effort and build ten more orphan homes. This vision became the Global Orphan Project, which now supports dozens of orphan villages in countries all around the world.[19]

On one early trip, the GO Project team realized orphan care alone was now too small of a vision. The team realized firsthand what the *Wall Street Journal* noted, "Many children in orphanages here aren't orphans at all, but have been given up by their desperately poor families."[20] Mothers were giving their children to be raised by strangers, rather than watching their children die of starvation.

For Global Orphan Project, it was a natural process to expand from orphan care to orphan *prevention*. GO Project has now partnered with local churches to strengthen vulnerable families, as well as providing education and economic development for the communities. The creation of economic development meant starting multiple charity enterprises.

The first enterprise, called the GO Fund (a unique impact investment fund managed by GO), helps start and operate businesses, creating dignified employment among the poor, and generates profits to help pay for orphan care.

The oldest and most robust of the ministry enterprises established by GO is The GO Exchange. The GO Exchange is a boutique collection of products, like Sseko sandals, jammies, jewelry, and purses—made in the communities served by orphan villages.

The product purchases from around the world mean moms and dads have income to keep their children at home with them. The profits also go to caring for orphans, while simultaneously reducing the number of orphans in a community. It's a perfect picture of charity enterprise in action.

Telling the story of Global Orphan Project in hindsight sounds so simple, but the journey was difficult and confusing at times, especially at the beginning. The GO Project leadership pressed through the confusion and surrounded themselves with a team of advisors from business, law, and nonprofit fields. Together they planned, worked hard, learned from their mistakes, adjusted their plans, and worked even harder until measurable success could be celebrated.

If you stand at the beginning of your charity enterprise journey and find it all too daunting, take hope. The following pages will give you much of the framework needed for success.

Prelaunch Planning

No matter how clever or resourceful, no one can do effective charity enterprise alone. Assemble a team with the expertise to help you in the prelaunch phase. The team you put together need not be the same people who carry out the day-to-day plans; but your team should have passion for your cause and time to invest—at least a few hours over the course of three to six months.

Build an advisory team with diverse backgrounds. A good mix might include individuals experienced in running a business, an accountant or CFO who can help with financial modeling, and people with an intimate knowledge of the context of your charity enterprise. Seek out both insiders and people with fresh perspectives.

Before starting a charity enterprise, your team should take time to ask and answer crucial questions. First, can the enterprise begin within an existing nonprofit or does it need to be a separate company with its own leadership? If it needs to be separate, should it be a nonprofit, tax-exempt entity, or a traditional for-profit business? If it will be a for-profit business, what type of corporate form—LLC, corporation, B-corporation, etc.—will best support its growth? Finally, what will be the nature of the relationship between the existing nonprofit and the new charity enterprise? The following points are a guide to help make those decisions.

Most people I have talked to over the years start with the assumption that a new entity must be created before moving forward. Starting a new company can be expensive and time-consuming, not to mention complicated to manage.

Generally, the charity enterprise can remain inside the nonprofit if the following is true:

1. The goals of the charity enterprise are closely aligned with the mission of the nonprofit;

2. The nonprofit's culture supports the creation of the charity enterprise ;

3. The nonprofit will be able to fund the startup with existing capital or with donations; and

4. The activities of the charity enterprise will not subject the nonprofit to liability.

These are simply factors to consider, and the absence of one element does not necessitate separating the charity enterprise from the nonprofit. Let's consider each of the factors listed above.

1. The goals of the charity enterprise are closely aligned with the mission of the nonprofit.

Empowerment Exchange, the charity enterprise introduced earlier, operates as a single organization because its revenue-generating activity is so related to the function of the charity that it didn't make sense to run two organizations. With goals like economic empowerment, job training, improved incomes for women in impoverished environments,

31

Empowerment Exchange could not accomplish its charitable goals without its business activities.

It is useful to introduce a bit of technical jargon here. We need to understand the phrase "exempt purpose" and determine whether the charity enterprise you are considering fits within that purpose. The IRS grants tax exemption to nonprofits whose stated goals and activities compose an "exempt purpose." The exempt purpose is a set of religious, charitable, scientific, or educational goals for which an organization is founded. A nonprofit's organizing documents—its Articles of Incorporation, bylaws, and Form 1023 (tax-exempt application to the IRS)—list its exempt purposes.

For Empowerment Exchange, the exempt purpose is charitable, specifically poverty relief through job training and economic development.

In order to keep a charity enterprise within the walls of your existing nonprofit, it must contribute importantly to the furtherance of your exempt purpose. Too much non-exempt activity can lead to trouble with the IRS. An organization may need to amend its organizing documents to accommodate the changes that have taken place over time or to fit with a new charity enterprise.

If the goals of your charity enterprise, like those of Empowerment Exchange's revenue-generating activities, are interdependent with your charitable purpose, the case is strong for keeping those activities in-house.

On the other hand, if the activity will be only tangentially related to the nonprofit's pursuit of its charitable purposes, it may be better to push the charity enterprise into a separate entity. Consider the example of Brother in Blue whose full story is below.

Mission Alignment: Brothers in Blue Reentry

I first met Jerry Ruzicka, Executive Director of Brothers in Blue Reentry ("BIB"), at a turbulent time in their ministry. BIB is a prison outreach ministry that began in the Kansas prison system as the InnerChange Freedom Initiative (IFI) and was part of Chuck Colson's Prison Fellowship Ministries.

Jerry and his team brought a curriculum and counseling program to Lansing Correctional Facility, while Prison Fellowship provided the funding and administration. After ten years of this partnership, Prison Fellowship hit financial hurdles and had to pull out of Kansas.

Rather than walk away from the success they'd seen, the two full-time and one part-time employees of BIB kept up their regular programs in the prisons and worked quickly to learn fundraising and basic nonprofit management. With help from their board, plus lots of their own hard work and determination, they were able to replace most of the funding that Prison Fellowship provided in just three years time.

Then the prison warden at Lansing called with an offer. He liked the BIB team and their curriculum because the participants of the program became model citizens of Lansing and stayed out of prison after release. The warden's offer included potential for funding if the Brothers would consider taking over the prison's café, which provided food service to visitors.

Immediately, Jerry saw it as a great opportunity. The café could provide needed revenue while expanding their ability to minister to the families and friends of prisoners. They accepted the warden's offer and set about learning all they needed in order to operate the café with excellence.

Jerry and the inmates who manage the café report serving about six hundred people each week. The café employees are gaining skills through training, customer service, and experience in restaurant management.

Running the prison's café program certainly enhances their ministry opportunities, but wasn't a prerequisite for accomplishing BIB's goals with the inmates. In this situation, the charity enterprise could easily be split from the nonprofit or dropped into a subsidiary if the other factors in this list above warrant it.

2. The nonprofit's culture supports the creation of the charity enterprise.

Unless the nonprofit's existing people and culture will support the success of the charity enterprise, the ME should be established outside the existing nonprofit.

One nonprofit we spoke with recently began a for-profit initiative and promptly had several key employees walk away. For these employees charging a fee for any of the nonprofit's services (even for those who could afford to pay for them) was antithetical to the organization's mission. Personnel issues can have a huge impact on whether it is advisable for a nonprofit to keep revenue generation in-house or create a separate identity. Employees of the nonprofit may feel a sense of loyalty to a more traditional social sector, using donations and nothing else to fuel operations.

Even if everyone is willing to venture into revenue generation, change is hard. Starting a new initiative inside an existing company involves change. Starting a new revenue-generating initiative requires more risk tolerance, faster innovation, and a different commitment to financial results than exists in many nonprofit cultures. Without these key elements, the charity enterprise may see disappointing results. Also, new employees who come from a business background to work within the charity enterprise may be frustrated by the slower, shared decision-making structures of most nonprofits.

If you do decide to separate the charity enterprise from the nonprofit, use care to avoid damaging the existing culture and brand. Maintaining a single organizational culture across two separate entities can be very difficult. Achieving consistency across two sets of employees and two different operations isn't easy.

R. Todd Johnson, an attorney participating in a webinar sponsored by Morrison & Foerster law firm, has a wealth of experience with social entrepreneurs and nonprofits. Johnson said that some nonprofits want to create a "one-hat brand," and that takes a lot of creative work when the organization's identity is bifurcated. But it can be done. National Geographic, for example, is seen as one brand—National Geographic. But it is actually made up of two entities—a nonprofit and a for-profit. Johnson said that he is working with a tandem nonprofit and for-profit to align the incentives for employees at both entities by designating a pool of the for-profit's equity to be distributed to the nonprofit employees if and when the for-profit is sold.

3. The nonprofit will be able to fund the startup with existing capital or with donations.

How will the charity enterprise be funded? Can the nonprofit use existing capital and resources to get the new venture to break even? If not, can the nonprofit leadership raise sufficient donations without endangering existing fundraising efforts?

If not, the charity enterprise needs to start as a separate entity.

A nonprofit can open the door to greater investment by creating a subsidiary with stock or other equity opportunities. If a for-profit entity is created, it can offer competitive compensation to attract the best employees. Plus, donors may be willing to give more than usual if they know it is going to contribute to financial sustainability.

4. The activities of the charity enterprise will not subject the nonprofit to liability.

Housing a revenue-generating activity in a separate entity may protect the nonprofit from serious liability. The greater the risk posed to the nonprofit assets, the better it may be to create a separate entity. To determine the liability exposure of a certain activity, ask yourself, "How could this go wrong?" When considering this question, remember that liability can take the form of financial, legal, or simple reputation risk. Good insurance coverage can take care of financial risk. Proper planning and structure can mitigate legal risks.

The last form of risk is more difficult to estimate and guard against. If supporters of a ministry form a negative view of a related charity enterprise, they may walk away from their support of the nonprofit as well. A strong public relations plan and donor outreach can help prevent this from happening. It is certainly worth considering the risks before launching a charity enterprise.

Considering the Costs of a Separate Structure

To state the obvious, it is more expensive to run two entities, or two brands, than one. Tandem legal structures can be incredibly expensive. The legal issues associated with moving assets from one entity to the other alone can be great. At the formation and governance stages, each organization may need its own attorneys to avoid conflicts of interest. Some nonprofits have been able to locate attorneys who are willing to do this work pro bono, but their willingness to invest hundreds of hours in one tandem legal structure is probably more the exception than the rule.

Scaled In

If the ultimate goal is to operate a charity enterprise as a separate endeavor, it may be best to start within an existing nonprofit structure. In other words, incubate the revenue-generating activities within the nonprofit and spin it out when the model proves itself or other factors necessitate separation. Field-testing the idea of the charity enterprise, without having to go through the expense of creating a new entity, can save a charity enterprise much time when it finally launches on its own.

iDonate, the business that I worked with during my time at National Christian Foundation Heartland, was founded this way. Bill High, the CEO of NCFH, recognized the need for helping nonprofits accept all forms of donations and began processing car donations on their behalf. This allowed iDonate to get off the ground quickly. Bill and the team learned much in this time. Most importantly, they learned what nonprofits really need and how to bring products that their target audience will find valuable. Within a few years, the company had grown large enough to be spun out into a separate organization with its own leadership.

Like NCFH and iDonate, your organization may choose to incubate a charity enterprise to get started quickly and begin learning firsthand what the market needs so you can iterate products as fast as possible.

CHAPTER 5

CHARITY ENTERPRISE IN ACTION

"Twenty years from now you will be more disappointed by the things that you didn't do than by the ones you did do. So throw off the bowlines. Sail away from the safe harbor. Catch the trade winds in your sails. Explore. Dream. Discover." —Mark Twain

Mission Adelante is a thriving charity enterprise in Kansas City, Kansas. They work with Latino and Bhutanese communities to build, in their words, a community "where immigrants and others are thriving and using their gifts together to transform their neighborhood and the world for the glory of Jesus Christ." They do this through discipleship, equipping leaders, and multiplying house churches.

The work began in 2005 when Jarrett and Kristen Meek returned from years as missionaries in Bolivia. Shortly after returning to Kansas City, they assembled a team of friends who had a similar heart for immigrants and began planning the launch of a new ministry. After relocating to an urban neighborhood with a significant immigrant population, the Meeks began meeting their neighbors and learning about the needs of the community. They started a Bible study, a kids program, English-as-a-Second-Language program, and even a church.

Nine years later, the team of Mission Adelante realized how transforming a community also meant fostering economic development. Mission Adelante assembled a team of business leaders for their board and a fan club of financial supporters. They settled on the idea of a thrift store in their neighborhood, staffed by the community they served. The thrift store would provide revenue for the ministry and job opportunities for the immigrant population in their community. This newly assembled team of business leaders and financial supporters set about building a business plan and created an income generating business through the process of opening this charity enterprise.

Today, Adelante Thrift is open and serving the Mission Adelante community. The creation of this new ministry enterprise did face some struggles. The obstacles, and the way the team overcame them, can be instructive for those just embarking on the charity enterprise road. The challenges fall into a few general categories and while Mission Adelante didn't face all of these hurdles, we will use their story for examples where appropriate.

Waiting

Two years after assembling a special team to launch the thrift store, the Adelante team couldn't find a suitable location for the project and they were about to give up. Jarrett and his team were seasoned ministry and business leaders, many of them with experience starting an organization from scratch. They had the degrees and experience, and their idea was solid, so what happened?

There are two lessons in this story. The first is a practical issue, the second a bit more ephemeral, but equally true, spiritual struggle.

Practical Lesson

On the practical issue, Jarrett explained that even though he lived in the neighborhood for years, he didn't realize how difficult it would be to find a large retail space of suitable quality. The city of Kansas City, Kansas, that is home to Mission Adelante has seen redevelopment in the past few years but much of that redevelopment hadn't reached the Adelante neighborhoods. The first location they visited seemed perfect, except for a leaky roof, broken HVAC system, and a landlord unwilling to talk with the team. They quickly moved on from that location, but nothing else seemed to work.

After two years of searching, Mission Adelante was ready to stop. They decided to set a deadline for finding a location. If they couldn't find a suitable location within their new time frame, they would table the project. Thankfully, the landlord from the first location changed his mind and signed a letter of intent just a few days before their deadline.

The lesson from Adelante Thrift's experience: spend time at the outset considering the unique assets and potential liabilities of your ministry and its related charity enterprise. But even with all great planning, expect hurdles and prayerfully and persistently wait through them.

It is possible the team might not have found a suitable property in the time allowed. A two-year search may have been an indication that their plan wasn't going to come to fruition. By setting a deadline, the project did not become an albatross, preventing the ministry from moving forward on other important initiatives.

Sometimes even the best plan and most skilled team run into unforeseeable market conditions. It takes skill to discern the right time to cut one's losses.

Spiritual Lesson

When asked what it seemed God was doing in the community, and in the leadership of Adelante Thrift, during this time, Jarrett explained how the season of waiting was essential to their readiness to serve effectively.

A member of the business team describes his biggest lesson: "Here we had a bunch of business guys doing what business guys do without remembering our utter dependence on God. We realized we had to enter a deeper level of surrender to the Lord and His timing." God used this time of waiting to remind the Adelante team of this very important truth.

It is written all over Scripture, but Proverbs 19:21 says it well, "Many are the plans in a person's heart, but it is the LORD's purpose that prevails." Our excellent work done as unto the Lord delights His heart. But He does not need us to make His will come to fruition in the world. His purposes will prevail and it's up to us to choose to align ourselves with Him.

If your charity enterprise team finds itself in a season of waiting or up against a seemingly immovable obstacle, start with prayer. Shift dependence from your great plan, excellent team, and years of experience onto the One True God. Then get back to work, with faith and reliance on Him.

Balancing Ministry Goal and Profit Goals

During the two years of looking for a suitable location for the Adelante thrift store, Jarrett describes a conversation he often had with his team of business advisors.

"We went around and around about whether we should just rent space in a more-resourced community. Sure, we could find a space easily and possibly make more money, but we would lose the involvement of the Adelante community." Eventually, the team decided to stick to their original plan and secure a location in their neighborhood.

The build-out phase provided a great indication that they had made the right decision. A church partner from a suburb thirty minutes away from Mission Adelante held a drive to collect items for the initial inventory of the thrift store. Forty volunteers collected bags of clothing, boxes of toys, and even furniture. They filled one and a half 18-wheel semi-trucks. Then the volunteer coordinator called Jarrett aside and warned him they had considerably more donations than expected and didn't think they had enough volunteers to unload the trucks at the warehouse.

Jarrett began calling his friends from the neighborhood—the immigrants that Mission Adelante serves. An hour later, there were sixty volunteers at their warehouse unloading the trucks. Afterward, to celebrate, they had an impromptu worship service and potluck dinner. It was a beautiful picture of exactly what Mission Adelante hoped to accomplish with the thrift store—building community and empowering them to work for their own neighborhood development—and all this wouldn't have happened if the thrift store had moved to the suburbs.

Every charity enterprise will have a different balance of business and ministry. Most of the time, those goals will not be at odds. But occasionally, you will find they are in tension and a decision will force you to choose which goal to favor. There is no right answer that works for every charity enterprise.

For example, consider the café for prison visitors. They may encounter a situation where their business needs to close on Mondays to save costs, and allow their small team to rest and prepare for the rest of the week. Mondays are the slowest days for visitors in the prison, although some families may be inconvenienced by this closure. This demonstrates the tension between their business needs and their ministry goals.

In this situation, the cost to their ministry outreach is light—90 percent of visitors come to the prison on days the café will be open—and the gain in terms of their business needs is great—a day off for rest or office work.

Your charity enterprise will be different, but spend time at the outset considering how you may address these tensions. Determine, and even write out, the ministry goals and the business goals. Then determine what each needs for success. You may even consider ranking them in order of importance. This will help you decide when you find your ministry needs are in tension with your business needs.

Leadership and Counsel

A ministry and its related charity enterprise need strong leadership to preserve the core aspects of the ministry while launching a new initiative. No leadership team, no matter how dedicated and skilled, will have all the experience necessary for both. Perhaps you need to spend time immersed in learning about the industry of your enterprise. Or bring in a team of advisors who have lived in the world you are entering. This is why I wrote this book, and part of why Impact Investing Foundation exists.

In the case of Mission Adelante, they traveled to other cities to learn how similar ministries ran their thrift stores. They studied business plans and they called experts to advise them on the aspects of running a retail store.

As you assemble a team, consider an observation shared by the Mission Adelante team: *You cannot outsource ownership.* The people who have the most vested interests in the success of the charity enterprise need to be in a position of authority and responsibility. Someone needs to own the vision and guide it to fruition—whether it's the ministry CEO or a dedicated board member.

Furthermore, do not underestimate the time and effort involved in launching a startup. Before committing to it, consider the strengths of your existing team and consider areas where those strengths will need to be supplemented. You may need volunteers or perhaps additional staff. If you deploy existing staff to launch the enterprise, consider filling their previous roles, at least part-time, so as not to let the core aspects of the ministry lag.

Mission Adelante had dozens of volunteers and a committed board of advisors, but the launch of Adelante Thrift still taxed their staff resources. Expect the same at your ministry.

It's Your Turn

I hope this book has opened your eyes to a new model for ministry and social good. And I hope the stories have inspired you to take action.

You'll find additional information about the nuts and bolts of charity enterprise in the appendices that follow.

I look forward to hearing about your challenges and successes, for the glory of God!

Aimee Minnich

APPENDIX A

A NEW CHARITY OR TAXABLE ORGANIZATION?

If you've determined a separate entity will be needed, this appendix will give you the keys to get started. First, you will need to evaluate whether to establish the charity enterprise as a tax-exempt entity—a charity—or a taxable, for-profit business. Obviously, becoming a tax-exempt charity is attractive because you will not have to pay taxes on the profits from exempt activities. Furthermore, a charity does not have to worry as much about producing a profit to return to investors.

On the other hand, a for-profit business offers more flexibility because it is not subject to the stringent IRS rules that govern charities. To determine whether the charity enterprise can be conducted in a tax-exempt charity or a for-profit business, consider two issues: first, the activities of the charity enterprise; and second, the source of funding for the nonprofit.

To be a charity, the charity enterprise must be engaged in activities the IRS considers worthy of tax exemption, which are charitable, religious, scientific. Basically, if the activity would be subject to Unrelated Business Income Tax, the charity enterprise will not be eligible for tax exemption.

But even if the activity could be considered exempt, it doesn't necessarily mean the charity enterprise should become a tax-exempt charity.

Organizing as a for-profit business could allow the enterprise to raise more capital than if it were relying on donations. This is because, as the name implies, for-profits are funded by contributions from individuals, other corporations, or even foundations, in exchange for ownership and a share of net income. Charities are funded by contributions from donors who receive a tax-deduction in return.

A charity does not have owners and its profits must be retained in the charity to fund its religious, scientific, or other charitable work, or be distributed to other charities. Profits of a charity cannot be distributed to individuals or taxable businesses.

Therefore, to determine whether a new charity enterprise will be a charity or a for-profit business, it is necessary to look at how the initial funding will be raised. If the initial funding needs are low and the vision compelling enough, the charity enterprise could launch with just donations and be a tax-exempt charity.

If the new endeavor needs substantial funding, or is risky enough that contributors will want a share of the profits in exchange for their investment, then the charity enterprise needs to be a for-profit business. The only way to find out how investors will react is to ask them.

Meet with a small group of supporters who could potentially invest in, or donate to, the charity enterprise and ask their opinion. Venture capital folks call this "soft circling." This is not the time to actually ask for money, but rather ask for advice. Explain the concept of the charity enterprise and then ask, "Is this the kind of project you think people would donate to, or invest in?"

Hopefully, their answers will give the clarity needed to determine whether the charity enterprise can be organized as a charity or as a for-profit business.

The Process of Forming a Company

The discussion about the proper form for a new charity enterprise will be much easier with a basic understanding of how it works to form a new company or charity. People often use the terms *nonprofit* and *charity* interchangeably, but they actually refer to distinct steps in the process of becoming a tax-exempt entity.

The first step is to file a charter with the Secretary of State in whichever state you choose. This state filing confers to the new charity enterprise its separate legal identity from the individuals who are conducing its activities. States will recognize a business as a for-profit corporation, nonprofit corporation, limited liability company (LLC), limited partnership (LP), limited liability partnership (LLP), professional corporation (PC), and the list goes on. Most states allow these filings to be made online through the website of the Secretary of State, and they all charge a fee.

If a nonprofit corporation also wants tax-exempt status so that its income will not be taxed and contributions to it will be eligible for tax deductions, it must file an application with the IRS. This application is made on Form 1023, which asks for detailed information about the activities of the nonprofit, its leadership, the population it plans to serve, and on and on. The IRS will respond—within six weeks to eighteen months—granting tax exemption if the activities of the nonprofit meet the requirements set forth in Section 501(c)(3) of the Internal Revenue Code. Obviously, this is why some people refer to charities as 501(c)(3)s. The IRS states its criteria clearly, "To be tax-exempt under section 501(c)(3) of the Internal Revenue Code, an organization must be organized and operated exclusively for exempt purposes set forth in section 501(c)(3), and none of its earnings may inure to any private shareholder or individual."[21] This means the nonprofit primarily works to advance purposes that are charitable, religious, educational, scientific, literary, testing for public safety, fostering national or international amateur sports competition, and preventing cruelty to children or animals.[22] Furthermore, to be tax-exempt, any profits must stay in the entity and be used to fund its growth and cannot be distributed to anyone or anything besides other charities.

Type of Entity	Formation Document	Governing Document	What Owners Are Called	Advantages
Corporation	Articles of Incorporation	Bylaws	Shareholders	Limited liability for owners; traditional form of business with much case law further defining the rules
Partnership	None needed	None required or partnership agreement if desired	Partners	Easy to start; no separate taxation for the entity Beware: NO LIMIT ON LIABILITY FOR OWNERS
Limited Liability Partnership (LLC)	Articles of Organization	Operating Agreement	Members	Partnership taxation with liability protection for owners
Low-profit limited liability company	Same	Same	Same	Same; these are new corporate forms and some view them as attractive for marketing purposes

There is much more to say about how to operate a charity in compliance with these rules, but that's outside the scope of this book. For more information, check out the helpful resources the IRS has published on its website, starting with Publication 557.

For-Profit Corporate Forms

If the charity enterprise will not be organized as a charity, the legal steps to get started are fairly straightforward. First, someone must act on behalf of the ME to register with the state to have recognition that the ME is a separate legal entity. Second, ask the IRS for a tax identification number, which is required to open a bank account. Third, set up the governing documents.

For the first step, Registering with the State, there are many options for this type of entity. A company becomes an entity by filing the right paperwork with the Secretary of State's office in the desired state. Most people choose to form in the state where they live, but truly any state in the Union will be happy to collect a fee and issue a letter conferring legal identity on the organization. Delaware has historically been a favorite because its laws are friendly to business. Many other states, including my own home state of Kansas, have recognized the income potential of business formation and have loosened their laws to compete with Delaware. Some states offer a larger array of options; this section will focus on the most popular entity choices for charity enterprises.

Corporation

For many years, the only option for someone who wished to organize a business was to form a corporation. Corporations have shareholders and are formed by filing Articles of Incorporation with the state. These articles spell out the basic purposes of the corporation, who will be liable for its formation, and who will act as a representative for the corporation if it gets sued. People choose to form as a corporation mainly because they are familiar and one of the oldest types of entities. But the tax structure of corporations can be tricky.

The IRS presumes every corporation will be taxed as what people call a "C Corporation." The name refers to the section of the tax code that governs their taxation. C Corporations are what most people think of as basic or regular corporations. The entity is legally distinct from its owners and is taxed as a legal person separate from its owners. Thus, every dollar of profit in a C Corp is taxed twice, once at the corporate level and once when the profits are distributed to the owners. Why would anyone want that, you'd ask? The answer is long and complicated and a tax professional can explain the nuances to you. But for our purposes, let it be sufficient to say that generally, we would not want to consider a C Corporation unless certain Unrelated Business Income Tax issues are in play (see Appendix B or call for consulting).

If a charity enterprise wants to be a corporation and still avoid the two layers of taxation, then it needs to elect to be taxed as an S Corporation, or S Corp for short. This means it is structured the same as a C Corporation with shareholder owners, but it is taxed like a partnership where income generated by the S Corporation "passes through" to the individual owners who are then taxed on that income. Unlike in a C Corp, all the income of the S Corp shows up on the owners' personal tax returns, avoiding the double taxation of C Corps.

Because of the tax advantages of S Corps over C Corps, the IRS limits the types of entities that can own S Corps. The S Corporation can have only one hundred shareholders, none of whom may be foreign individuals, other corporations—unless those corporations are tax-exempt—or certain trusts.[23]

Another disadvantage of becoming an S Corporation is all income received by a nonprofit owner from the S Corporation is taxable as unrelated business income.[24] This is true regardless of whether the income is generated by an unrelated business activity or if it is passive income usually excluded from unrelated business income. The same would be true of LLCs as well.

Benefit Corporation

Another emerging option is the benefit corporation. As of July 2013, nineteen states have enacted legislation, making the new corporate form available, and eleven others have introduced such legislation.[25] Benefit corporations are legally authorized and required to simultaneously pursue profit and social good. Although sharing a similar name, benefit corporations are not the same as B Corps (and may or may not be certified by B Lab as B Corps).

Some states offer similar corporate forms, such as the flexible purpose corporation (FPC) or social purpose corporation (SPC). Benefit corporations receive the same tax treatment as C Corporations, but are partially governed by different laws than a C or S Corporation.

As a corporate form, the benefit corporation could potentially better facilitate the transfer of funds or assets from the for-profit subsidiary to the nonprofit parent. Benefit corporations are created to pursue profit *and* social and environmental benefits. While the corporation is required to create a net positive impact on the environment and society, it can also include one or more specific public benefits. A specific public benefit could be, for example, to support a particular nonprofit organization.

Every state has somewhat different benefit corporation legislation, and there are still many gray areas surrounding the entity because it is so new, having been first recognized in 2010. Many within the legal community are uncertain as to how the entities will be run, when their directors may face liability, and how the entity will be taxed in the future. So any nonprofit looking at starting a benefit corporation should take time to thoroughly understand the issues unique to the entity and the applicable state legislation.

The taxation of a benefit corporation will be similar to regular corporations—either C Corp double taxation or S Corp pass-through taxation creating UBIT for the charity owners.

LLC

A charity enterprise could also become a limited liability company (LLC). All of these entities are pass-through entities (like the S Corporation), meaning income is taxed to the individual receiving it and not to the entity unless the LLC elects to be taxed as a C Corp with double tax.[26] The owners of an LLC are called "members," and if they are the ones that run it, then the LLC is called a manager-managed LLC. If, on the other hand, non-members are the ones in charge of the LLC's operations, that LLC would be classified as a manager-managed LLC.

A major benefit to the LLC as an entity is its incredible flexibility. The governing document for an LLC is called an Operating Agreement, and it is essentially a contract that can be tailored to the needs and wants of the members. For example, an owner with 60 percent of the vote can be allocated 40 percent of the profit—a helpful proposition if you want to bring in new investors with less control but a greater share of the profits. Not only do LLCs provide a great deal more flexibility than corporations, but they also provide their members with limited liability, unlike a partnership or sole proprietorship. So, in a sense, the LLC is the best of both worlds.

name="

L3C

At the beginning of the social enterprise movement, most social enterprises used regular corporate forms to pursue social good. They would amend the company's articles of incorporation and/or bylaws, or operating agreement in the case of an LLC. Since then, hybrid social enterprises have emerged. Hybrid social enterprises are legal entities that have a social mission encoded into their DNA, so to speak.

In the past few years, a few states have begun offering a new type of business entity specifically crafted to suit the duel purposes of social good and, secondarily, profit for investors. The L3C—or "low-profit limited liability company"—is intended to combine the mission of a nonprofit with the efficacy and perquisites of an LLC. Unless state statutes provide otherwise, the L3C is treated as an LLC for all legal and tax purposes.

There has, however, been significant debate regarding this entity. Although its creators wanted it to attract program-related investments from private foundations, the IRS has not issued the regulations to officially recognize this avenue.[27] There is also a great deal of disagreement over the L3C's usefulness.

Daniel S. Kleinberger, a prominent legal scholar, articulated his strong feelings on the subject, saying, "The L3C is an unnecessary and unwise contrivance, and its very existence is inherently misleading."[28] LLCs are already highly customizable and provide members with limited liability, and their Operating Agreements can be crafted to serve the desires of the members including making the LLC a primarily mission-driven organization.

Appendix B

Time to Talk Tax

You might have seen the title of this appendix and thought to yourself, *Oh, good, I can skip this one because we're a tax-exempt organization. It won't apply to me.*

Wrong. Just because an organization is exempt from taxes as a 501(c)(3) organization doesn't mean it can avoid taxes on all of its income, all the time.

"Well, that doesn't make sense," you say. "The concept of a tax-exempt organization paying taxes is an oxymoron." Mainly this is true, but for a few exceptions every nonprofit should know. With the goals of a level playing field for traditional for-profits and to make sure tax-exempt organizations focus on their mission, the IRS developed a set of rules to determine when a charity might have to pay taxes on its earned income.

Generally, a charity will have to pay taxes when the income it earns meets the definition of Unrelated Business Income ("UBI" for short). Income will be subject to tax if it is: (1) from a trade or business, (2) regularly conducted business, and (3) not substantially related to the organization's exempt purpose or function, except that the organization uses the profits derived from this activity.[29]

Trade or Business

What is a trade or business? The IRS definition is probably pretty close to what most would consider a trade or business: selling goods or performing services to produce income. Some trade or business activities are actually excluded from the IRC's definition of an unrelated trade or business, and so they escape taxation. The main exclusions apply when a trade or business is conducted by volunteers, exists for the sake of the organization's beneficiaries, involves the sale of donated product, or incorporates a variation of the game of bingo. When a trade or business activity falls into one of the descriptions below, it will not be classified as an unrelated trade or business and UBIT will not apply to the income it generates.

1. **Volunteer Labor:** The work performed in the trade or business activity is "substantially all" done without compensation.

2. **Convenience:** A trade or business is carried on to convenience its members, employees, or students in the case of a school. For example, a school that operates a cafeteria to serve lunch to its students would likely be exempt and its income not considered UBI.

3. **Sale of Donated Product:** The trade or business activity consists of selling merchandise that was "substantially all" donated to the organization. The classic example is a thrift store whose profits support a homeless shelter.

4. **Bingo:** Game night at church, anyone? When tax-exempt organizations include gaming in their activities, local, state, and federal laws may apply. For more information, see the additional resources listed under "Gaming" in Appendix C.[30]

What if instead of selling donated products, a nonprofit sells products resulting from what it does—in other words, from its exempt purpose functions? The answer is: it depends. The IRS has said, "If the product is sold in substantially the same state it is in when the exempt functions are completed," then the activity is not an unrelated trade or business and UBIT doesn't apply.[31] Such rules might exempt income from the sale of clothing made by residents of an in-patient addiction recovery center, where an important part of the program is training residents for manufacturing jobs.

Regularly Carried On

Knowing whether the activity is "regularly carried on" is a bit less clear. The IRS looks at several factors, including the frequency and continuity of the activity. Another important factor is whether the nonprofit pursues the activity in a manner similar to comparable activities of non-exempt organizations. If you've ever bought more Thin Mints than needed because you didn't know how long the Girl Scout troop would have them in stock, then you've been affected by this rule. One reason the Girl Scouts only sell cookies for a few weeks each year is so they can escape the "regularly carried on" aspect of the UBI definition.

Substantially Related

Analyzing whether a trade or business is unrelated to an organization's exempt purpose is like looking for strings that connect the two. To know if there are strings connecting the activity to the mission, ask this question: Does the business activity contribute importantly to accomplishing the purposes for which the organization is exempt? If so, the activity *is* substantially related to the organization's charitable purpose and the income it generates is not subject to UBIT. If not, then the activity falls within the IRC's definition of an unrelated trade or business and the income it generates will be subject to UBIT.[32]

This is not a simple "yes" or "no" question. To answer it, we have to look at each individual situation and analyze whether there are or are not enough strings connecting the trade or business activity to the organization's exempt purpose.

Size and Extent of Trade

Two important factors are the size and extent of the trade or business activities. The size and extent of the activities should be considered relative to the nature and extent of the organization's exempt purpose. The IRS has stated that "to the extent an activity is conducted on a scale larger than is reasonably necessary to perform an exempt purpose, it does not contribute importantly to the accomplishment of the exempt purpose."[33]

Figure 4.1 offers a graphic interpretation of this. The outermost ring contains the portion of the trade or business activities that are not reasonably necessary for the performance of an exempt purpose—the charitable, religious, scientific, or educational purpose for which the organization was granted tax exemption. Because these activities do not contribute importantly to the accomplishment of the exempt purpose, they would be classified as unrelated trades or businesses. Income that results from activities in this outermost ring will be classified as unrelated business income and thus be subject to UBIT.

When determining whether an activity contributes importantly to the furtherance of an exempt purpose (and is therefore substantially related), there are some important principles to keep in mind. First, an activity is not substantially related just because it funds the organization's fulfillment of its exempt purpose. This income flow doesn't count as a string connecting the trade or business to the exempt purpose.

Similarly, just because an asset or facility is used for both exempt purposes and for conducting commercial activities doesn't mean the commercial activity is substantially related. The IRS gave the example of a museum auditorium that is used for public education and as a movie theater when the museum is closed. The movie theater business activity does not contribute importantly to the museum's exempt purpose by virtue of the auditorium's dual use.

In the same vein, the business activity would not be substantially related to the museum's exempt purpose just because it relied in some way on the goodwill or other intangible asset generated by the museum's exempt activities.

Passive Income Exclusion

To this point, the analytical focus has been on the trade or business activity. Now our focus turns to the actual items of income generated by the activity. Some items of income are actually excluded from unrelated business taxable income.

To clarify, exclusions are different from deductions and exemptions. For illustrative purposes, imagine each item of income as a soccer ball and all unrelated business income (the income subject to UBIT) as the net. When an exclusion applies, the soccer ball misses the net entirely, meaning that item of income is not ever classified as unrelated business income. When a deduction or an exemption applies, a soccer ball that has entered the net then exits the net and doesn't count toward the "score" (aka, taxable income, or the amount from which initial tax payable is calculated).

The main UBIT exclusion applies to what is referred to as "passive income," or income the nonprofit does not work to produce. Passive income consists of dividends, interest, annuities, payments on securities loans, and other substantially similar items of income a nonprofit earns on its investments. These items of passive income are not to be included in a nonprofit's unrelated business income according to Section 512(b) of the IRC.

But Wait! There's an Exception to the Exclusion

There is an exception to the passive income exclusion that should be noted. Nonprofits can own part of a for-profit company and the income it receives from that investment will be considered passive unless the nonprofit owns "too much" of the for-profit venture. If the nonprofit is a controlling organization, then the entity owned is referred to as a controlled organization. If the controlling organization receives or accrues passive income generated by the controlled entity, that income must be classified as unrelated business income.[34] The first step in determining whether this exception applies is to see if the nonprofit receiving or accruing the passive income is a controlling organization. To know that, we must ask one of three questions as highlighted below.

If the answer to the applicable question in Figure 4.2 is "yes," the entity is controlled.[35] Because the entity is a controlled organization, the nonprofit receiving or accruing passive income from it is a controlling organization and cannot exclude it from its unrelated business income.[36]

Too Much Taxable Income?

If a charity has too much taxable income, the IRS worries that the enterprise is operating too much like a regular business and ignoring its tax-exempt purpose. For that reason, the presence of too much unrelated business income jeopardizes the organization's exempt status.

How much is too much? Unfortunately, there are no bright-line rules for determining how much taxable income would revoke a charity's exempt status. Some have said an organization need not worry if its unrelated business income accounts for no more than 10 to 25 percent of its total income.[37] In some private letter rulings, however, the IRS has allowed up to 50 percent, and even up to 95 or 100 percent in a few instances.[38]

If more than 25 percent of a nonprofit's income is unrelated business income, it needs to evaluate its activities using the "commensurate in scope" test. One expert explained the test, saying "an organization may receive a significant amount of unrelated business income...as long as it carries out charitable programs that are commensurate in scope with its financial resources."[39] The IRS will look at the percentage *and* the overall activities of the exempt organization to see how its related and unrelated activities compare. A higher percentage of taxable income would be acceptable for an organization that has significant charitable activities.

If a Charity Is Tax-Exempt, Why Pay Income Tax?

The tax code is one of Congress's greatest public policy tools. By taxing some activities and giving tax relief for others, Congress can encourage the activities it deems to be in the overall public interest while discouraging the ones it doesn't like (at least that's the theory).

The notion that tax-exempt charities exist because lawmakers believe certain activities like education, poverty relief, scientific research, and low-cost medical care should be incentivized with tax exemption. The unrelated business income tax exists to eliminate unfair advantage of a charity when it's competing against taxable businesses in areas outside the charitable realm.

This is accomplished by subjecting the unrelated business activities of tax-exempt organizations to the same taxes as the non-exempt businesses with which they compete. Congress and the IRS are paying more attention to unrelated business income tax as a potential source of new revenue as well.

What Does This Really Mean for Charities?

Sometimes nonprofits are required to pay income tax. Knowing when tax is triggered is central to the charity enterprise discussion because it will influence how a nonprofit generates income. As a general rule, when a nonprofit generates revenue in a way that isn't sufficiently connected to its exempt purpose, that revenue is subject to UBIT. Below is a quick guide to determining if an activity will be taxed.

Decision Matrix: Is It Subject to Tax?

The following is my attempt to put the entirety of tax law related to nonprofit income on one page. It's just a guide to aid understanding and not meant as legal advice.

Is it taxable?

Start here — Is it a trade or business (selling goods or performing services to produce

no / yes

Is it excluded?
- volunteer labor
- service solely to convenience members/employees/students of the charity
- selling mostly donated items

yes → NOT taxable

no

Is it regularly carried on (conducted in the same manner as a similar for-profit entity)?

yes

Is it substantially related to the exempt purpose (conducting the trade or business helps the organization accomplish its exempt purpose?)

Is the charity a "controlling entity" with respect to the organization producing the interest, dividend or capital gains?

Is it passive income (rent, royalties, dividends, interest?)

Is it done on a scale much larger than necessary to accomplish exempt purpose?

NOT taxable

Taxable

Taxable

This is just a teaching aid, not intended as tax or legal advice

Don't forget to file!

If a nonprofit generates more than one thousand dollars in income from business activities that are unrelated to its exempt purposes, the organization must file IRS Form 990-T. This form is to be filed in addition to (and not instead of) any others required by the IRS.

Appendix C

Additional Resources

The growing field of charity enterprise involves the blending of classic business disciplines, startup methodology, and nonprofit basics. Rather than try to write a comprehensive treatise on all those areas, the following represents the best resources I've seen in each of the categories:

- **Startup:** Getting a new venture off the ground is tough. Some quote the success rate as low as 10 percent for new businesses. The methodology of Lean Startup is transforming the landscape of startup businesses. Most business schools have adopted their curriculum to include these principles. Read *The Lean Startup* by Eric Ries or visit his website, theleanstartup. com.

- **Disciplined Growth:** If you already have a successful ministry, adding a charity enterprise to the list of goals to accomplish can be tricky. *The 4 Disciplines of Execution* is a book and set of tools created by Franklin Covey to help teams execute on their most important plan in the midst of the daily whirlwind. Buy the book or watch the videos at www.the4disciplinesofexecution. com/.

- **Counsel:** The organization I've help found, Impact Investing Charitable Foundation, can help your charity enterprise get off the ground. Impact Foundation exists to help start, grow, and invest in businesses with a triple-bottom line. Those businesses may be inside of or totally separate from a nonprofit. We offer no-cost training to nonprofits as part of our charitable purpose. Visit www.ImpactFoundation.org.

Aimee Minnich

About Aimee

Aimee Minnich serves as co-founder and general counsel of Impact Foundation. After practicing law in Kansas City, she joined the National Christian Foundation Heartland serving in a variety of roles, including president/general counsel.

Aimee has been drawn into the world of impact investing because she saw how charity enterprise has the power to do what charity alone cannot.

Aimee graduated with honors from Rockhurst University and the University of Kansas School of Law. She and her husband, Marshall, have three adorable, high-energy kids.

www.ImpactFoundation.org

NOTES

Aimee Minnich

(ENDNOTES)

1 http://www.dailymail.co.uk/news/article-2092425/Haiti-earthquake-How-donated-billions-INCREASED-poverty-corruption.html

2 The Four Lenses Strategic Framework, Nonprofit with Income-Generating Activities. (Accessed July 18, 2013.) http://www.4lenses.org/setypology/iga.

3 Suzanne Perry, "The Stubborn 2% Giving Rate: Even as More Fundraisers Seek Donations, Americans Don't Dig Deeper," The Chronicle of Philanthropy (June 17, 2013), http://philanthropy.com/article/The-Stubborn-2-Giving-Rate/139811/. The number six years earlier was 2.2% six years earlier, and 2.3% five years before that. That's a .3% shift in eleven years.

4 Lucy Bernholz publishes a forecast for the social sector every year, and her forecast for 2012 anticipated philanthropic giving to remain as stagnant as it had in previous years. Well, she was right.

5 Fry, Richard, "This year Millennials will overtake Baby Boomers," Pew Research Center. (Accessed January 16, 2015.) http://www.pewresearch.org/fact-tank/2015/01/16/this-year-millennials-will-overtake-baby-boomers/.

6 http://online.barrons.com/article/SB50001424052748703889404578440972842742076.html#articleTabs_article%3D1. 1/16/2014

7 Research Area: Nonprofit Sector, The Urban Institute. Accessed July 22, 2013.) http://www.urban.org/nonprofits/more.cfm.

8 Katie L. Roeger, et al., The Nonprofit Almanac 2012 (2012), highlights available at http://www.urban.org/books/ nonprofit-almanac-2012/index.cfm. In 2012, 2.6 million nonprofits were estimated to exist in the United States.

9 http://www.pewresearch.org/daily-number/the-millennial-count/. (Accessed January 16, 2014.)

10 https://www.barna.org/barna-update/millennials/612-three-spiritual-journeys-of-millennials.html#prodigals. (Accessed January 16, 2014.)

11 http://www.morganstanley.com/sustainableinvesting/pdf/ Sustainable_Signals.pdf.

12 For a more detailed discussion of metrics in the nonprofit sector, see Appendices.

13 http://www.bcorporation.net. (Accessed January 10, 2014.)

14 http://www.relevantmagazine.com/reject-apathy/11-cool-products-are-making-difference.

15 Brady Josephson, "Why Amazon Is Smiling and Charities May Be Losing." http://www.huffingtonpost.com/brady-josephson/why-amazon-is-smiling-and_b_4360405.html.

16 http://economix.blogs.nytimes.com/2013/08/20/the-future-of-the-charitable-deduction/?_r=0, The Future of the Charitable Deduction.

17 Suzanne Perry, "Senate Hearing Produces Sharp Opinions About Future of Tax Breaks for Charitable Gifts." http://philanthropy.com/article/A-Capitol-Hill-Debate-on-the/129461/.

18 Emphasis added.

19 This story is adapted from "The Global Orphan Project Founder's Story" on their website at https://goproject.org/wp-content/uploads/2012/03/ FoundersStory.pdf.

20 WSJ, February 3, 2010, "Missionary Case Illuminates Plight of Haiti's Orphans."

21 http://www.irs.gov/Charities-%26-Non-Profits/Charitable-Organizations/Exemption-Requirements-Section-501(c)(3)-Organizations. (Accessed January 8, 2014.)

22 http://www.irs.gov/Charities-&-Non-Profits/Charitable-Organizations/Exempt-Purposes-Internal-Revenue-Code-Section-501(c)(3). (Accessed January 8, 2014.)

23 Although some sources point to IRC § 1361(b)(1)(B) to say that nonprofit organizations cannot create and S corporations, according to 26 U.S.C. 1361(c)(6) all organizations that are tax-exempt under 501(a) (which would include 501(c)(3) nonprofits) can be shareholders in an S or C corporation.

24 26 U.S.C. § 512(e) (2012).

25 B Corporation, Legislation, http://www.bcorporation.net/what-are-b-corps/legislation (Accessed July 23, 2013.)

26 It should be noted LLCs can choose to be treated like corporations, but most do not elect this tax treatment. Robert A. Wexler & Stephanie L. Petit, Revenue-Generating Activities of Charitable Organizations: Legal Issues, Alder & Colvin n.51 (2006), available at http://www.adlercolvin.com/pdf/revenue_generating_activities/AC_Web_Docs--Revenue_Generating_Activities_(00160207).pdf.

27 Kelly Kleiman, "L3C" Spells "Caveat Emptor," Stanford Social Innovation Review (March 18, 2011). http://www.ssireview.org/blog/entry/l3c_spells_caveat_emptor.

28 Daniel S. Kleinberger, A Myth Deconstructed: The "Emperor's New Clothes" on the Low-Profit Limited Liability Company, 35 Del. J. Corp. L. 879, 879 (2010), available at http://www.ssireview.org/blog/entry/l3c_spells_caveat_emptor.

29 Publication 598

30 Unrelated Business Income Tax Exceptions and Exclusions, IRS (Apr. 22, 2013), http://www.irs.gov/Charities-&-Non-Profits/Charitable-Organizations/Unrelated-Business-Income-Tax-Exceptions-and-Exclusions.

31 IRS, Publication 598: Tax on Unrelated Business Income of Exempt Organizations 4 (2012), available at www.irs.gov/pub/irs-pdf/p598.pdf.

32 26 U.S.C. § 513(a) (2012).

33 IRS, Publication 598: Tax on Unrelated Business Income of Exempt Organizations 3–4 (2012), available at www.irs.gov/pub/irs-pdf/p598.pdf.

34 There are exceptions to the exclusion, and exceptions to the exceptions to the exclusion, but we won't delve into those here.

35 This section is adapted from a description of Section 513 rules on the IRS website. IRS, Form 990-T—Organizations with Controlled Entities (April 29, 2013). http://www.irs.gov/Charities-&-Non-Profits/Form-990-T-%E2%80%93-Organizations-with-Controlled-Entities.

36 26 U.S.C. § 513(b)(13) (2012).

37 Dawn Olivardia, Michelle Mechior, Scott Thompsett, So You Think You're Tax Exempt: Unrelated Business Income, Grant Thornton, LLP Powerpoint slide 45 (June 28, 2011); Emily Chan, The Profitable Side of Nonprofits – Part I: Earned Income, Nonprofit Law Blog (May 6, 2011), http://www.nonprofitlawblog.com/home/2011/05/the-profitable-side-of-nonprofits-part-i-earned-income.html.

38 Robert A. Wexler, Legal Framework For Earned Income 22–23, n.36–37 (2007), available at http://www.adlercolvin.com/pdf/revenue_generating_activities/AC_Web_Resource-Legal_Framework_for_Earned_Income_(00160444).PDF; Dawn Olivardia, Michelle Mechior, Scott Thompsett, So You Think You're Tax Exempt: Unrelated Business Income, Grant Thornton, LLP Powerpoint slide 45 (June 28, 2011). Note that private letter rulings do not have any precedential value, meaning they cannot be relied upon by anyone other than the party to whom the ruling was issued.

39 Robert A. Wexler, Legal Framework For Earned Income 22 (2007), available at http://www.adlercolvin.com/pdf/revenue_generating_ activities/AC_Web_Resource-Legal_Framework_for_Earned_ Income_(00160444).PDF

Aimee Minnich